INNER KNOWING
Heart Connection to the Divine Within

Mary Pat Magde

IMAGINEWE
Publishers™
ImagineWe Publishers
A Global Publisher

If you purchase this book without a cover you should be aware that this book may have been stolen property and reported as "unsold and destroyed" to the publisher. In such a case, neither the author nor the publisher has received any payment for this "stripped book."

IMAGINEWE
Publishers™

Published by ImagineWe, LLC
ImagineWe Publishers
247 Market Street, Suite 201
Lockport, NY 14094
United States
www.imaginewepublishers.com

ISBN: 979-8-9917997-3-7 (Paperback)
ISBN: 979-8-9917997-4-4 (Hardback)
Library of Congress Control Number: 2025900899

© 2024 ImagineWe, LLC

Author Photo by Paula Zack

All rights reserved. No part of this publication may be reproduced, stored in a retrieval system or transmitted in any form or by any means, electronic, mechanical, photocopying, recording or otherwise without the prior permission of the publisher or in accordance with the provisions of the Copyright, Designs and Patents Act 1988 or under the terms of any license permitting limited copying issued by the Copyright Licensing Agency. For permissions, write to the publisher "Attention: Permissions Coordinator" at info@imaginewepublishers.com.

For more information about publishing with IWP, please visit the website listed above. To shop our selection of books and merchandise you can visit: shop.imaginewepublishers.com

This book is dedicated to my wonderful husband Doug, for all his love, support, and encouragement.

I also dedicate this book to all who are on their own unique spiritual journey of discovery.

Acknowledgments

Thank you to my family and friends who have supported me on my journey of life here.

A special thank you to many of my spiritual teachers in the past few years that have challenged me to grow and evolve.

Mike Dooley who opened the door for me through his books and several online courses that expanded my spiritual awareness.

Davidji who taught me the benefits and practice of meditation.

Sara Landon who taught "The Art of Channeling" course that changed my life.

Michael Sandler who taught Automatic Writing to help expand my channeling further.

Joanne Cary who channels deep wisdom and set up a supportive global community for us to learn and grow together.

Pamela Landolt Green who has taught me how to connect with angels.

Tracy Saqladi my spiritual mentor and Transference Healing teacher who helps me see things from a higher perspective, teaches me practical tools and encourages me to both continue to grow spiritually and empower myself.

An additional thank you to all of you who have been traveling on this spiritual journey of discovery with me these past few years in our weekly Channeling group, spiritual book clubs, and Master Empowerment Ascension group.

My Awakening Journey

My book of my channeled poetry and my photos, "Inner Knowing – Heart Connections to the Divine Within" is how my soul spoke to me on my journey and how Spirit wanted to communicate to the world.

I did not set out to write and publish a book. As far back as I can remember I have been a "seeker." I've been curious about life and spiritual growth. I've tried and experimented with various ways to expand my spiritual awareness. I have followed traditional avenues, then meditation, learning about angels and guides, channeling and automatic writing, Transference Healing and working with a spiritual mentor. In August 2021, I took an online course through Mike Dooley and Sara Landon called "The Art of Channeling Adventure" with daily videos/lessons and daily practices. This course changed my life!

Mary Pat Magde

Later in June 2022, I took another course again through Mike Dooley with Michael Sandler, "The 21-day Automatic Writing Adventure" course. With these courses, there was an option to join a private social media community group for those participating in these courses. It was a safe place to experiment and try channeling. We could post our channeled messages in this group, and receive support and encouragement. One co-participant in the "Art of Channeling" course and FB group was Joanne Cary. She set up a weekly practice channeling zoom group for people to share their channeling messages, written, spoken or energy transmission. I did not share a lot but I was able to sit in the energies of the group and learn. My channeling tends to come out in poetry form and I feel guided to take certain pictures in nature.

We are so much more than our physical bodies and limited minds. Channeling is a way to get in touch with your Higher Self, God, Source, Spirit, Christ Consciousness, Universe, Divine Self (what you name it doesn't matter). You take a few deep breaths, drop into your heart, and allow yourself to receive. Myself or anyone who channels are not special or unique. Everyone has access to this. We are all equal. People may have unique expressions of their personalities, but all are souls in physical form.

My channeling has primarily taken the form of written poetry. With my channeled photographs, I feel guided toward specific perspectives and moments. I feel most connected when walking in nature, embracing the beauty of the trees and the shifting seasons. Who knows if my channeling will remain in this form or evolve into something new? That's okay—it's a journey. My spirituality is always evolving.

Introduction: My Awakening Journey

Channeling is not "new." Artists, musicians, scientists, engineers, etc. are channeling their creations. Being "in the flow" of a conversation with a friend – when you just know those words coming out of you are not your own as they connect with others souls, that is channeling. Everyone finds their own unique journey in this life.

I hope the channeled messages in this book will remind you of who you are in truth…Remind you of your own Divinity within. Remind you that we are all connected, all One and connected to Source/God/Universe. This is a book that you can just open to any page, take in the message and photo.

Feel them.

Allow them to connect to you.

I hope you follow your own path to discover your inner Divinity and allow yourself to be seen in the world. Shine your unique light. You are not alone. You are loved. You are Divinely made and Divinely perfect. Remember who you are. You may relate to parts of my personal journey or not at all. That is fine.

Enjoy the poems and pictures as they are…

Why are you here?
What is your purpose?

What is it that only you
can bring to the world?

You are needed
Your impact matters
with your small or large gestures

You matter
You are vital
You are necessary

You are loved beyond measure

Expansion is happening with you and the world

Go with it

Waking in the night
is part of this shift in energy

Go with it

Write in the night next time this happens

You can find your roots and grounding like a tree

As tall trees can see for great distances – so can you gain higher perspectives

As trees are connected with each other and communicate with each other through signals and their root system
So can you feel the oneness to
others and everything and Source

Trees experience seasonal changes and growth
So, shall you
Accept the process of growth and change

Every season has its beauty shown in the trees
As it is with all of you

Smile, notice, and be grateful for each step

You are glorious beings interconnected to all

We love you

Inner Knowing: Heart Connections to the Divine Within

Appreciate
Appreciate the small things

A smile
A conversation with a friend
Christmas lights on a dark evening
Festive music
A nostalgic movie
Hot chocolate
Homemade cookies
A warm blanket
Strangers wishing each other Happy Holidays

A breath of fresh air
A deer meandering by
Dogs playing
Birds singing
The beauty of trees - bare or fully dressed

Look around
What do you
See?
Hear?
Smell?
Taste?
Touch?

In these small things,
moments, discover gratitude

Release
Release
Release
Old versions of yourself
that no longer serve you

You have the power and choice
to become NEW each moment

Now is the time to let go
See yourself in the NEW upgraded version
Feel it
Yes, that is who you truly are

Remember?

YES!

Be in kindness with everyone and everything
Be in kindness
Be Kind

Be in peace with everyone and everything
Be in peace
Be Peace

Be in joy with everyone and everything
Be in joy
Be Joy

Be in love with everyone and everything
Be in love
Be Love

Be in awareness with everyone and everything
Be in awareness
Be Awareness

Be all in this precious moment

See all that is enfolding for the good of all
Look for the light
It is there

Be the light for others
Create a positive change

Behold
Behold
Behold

Love remains always

Glory Glory Glory
for this moment in time

Glorious
Rejoice

Behold all the splendor
that surrounds you
and is inside of you

It is there
and always has been
Uncover it today

Mary Pat Magde

Receive
Get quiet
Very quiet
in stillness

Receive
All that we have to offer
You are always supported

Trust
Trust
Trust

Peace arrives
Joy arrives
Knowing arrives

All is well

We love you
We love you
We love you

All is well
Many issues are presenting themselves
for you to see, feel and experience
to then release what no longer serves you

Are these really mistakes you have made?
Didn't you make the best decision at
the time with the information you had?
So really all are lessons
Just awarenesses
Just places to "expand" in now

Release all judgment
Allow deep self-love

This is the lesson
This is the pathway
to deeper knowing

Mary Pat Magde

Breathe in loving kindness
Breathe out loving kindness

Breathe in loving kindness
Breathe out gratitude

What are you grateful for,
right now, in this moment?

Inner Knowing: Heart Connections to the Divine Within

You have deep magic within
You were born with it
You have had this through many lifetimes
Remember who you are

You are connected to all

You are the Universe
and the Universe is you

You are Divine Source
and Divine Source is you

You are wisdom
and wisdom is you

You are pure magic

There is no separation
All is One
and One is All

See it
Feel it
Be it
Believe it
Act it

Rest
Recharge
Release what no longer serves you anymore
What's no longer a part of you
Let go
Pause
Set intentions
of all you can be...desire
Of all you truly are
Of all that has always been deep inside
You remember...
Rebirth
Claim it now

Shine
Shine your light

Shine your light
even if it makes others uncomfortable

Be an example
Be you
Speak your truth
Be your truth

The time is now

You are right where you need to be
Continue to open and allow

Notice our signs, our whispers to your heart

Don't underestimate your power to
affect others with your light

Each encounter long or brief can be life-changing

Spread your light and love

We are always here with you

We love you beyond words

All is well

Now
You are loved
You are love
You are pure love
All those who crossed over love you
All those here love you
We love you

Love connects us all
Can you feel that?

Breathe in the LOVE

All is well, sweet child

No work to be done
No action

It is here now

Breathe

Feel it

All is well
(Notice the hearts in my picture, love from Source)

We haven't left you
We are always here

Just plug in
Yes like an electrical outlet
the electricity is always available

Be the plug and connect

Take time for silence and stillness
this may help you connect

Really you can connect at anytime
In the silence
In the noise
In the chaos

Just ask
We are always here

Here to support you and all

We love you

Mary Pat Magde

See the geese flying south
They instinctively know where to fly

So do we
Our hearts can guide us

Notice the trees
What lessons can we learn from them

Trees are beautifully dressed
in Spring, Summer and Fall
We can easily see
all that shows itself outward

Come the end of Fall and Winter
We can see the trunk and the beautiful
structure of the bare branches
Still, so much is happening inside
that we don't see

With each other, we see outward behavior,
glimpses of our naked soul yet
there is so much more inside

Honor the beauty outside, inside
and hidden in all
The glory of the Divine

Your voice
What do you want to say?

Why did you come here?
What can you offer
that no one else can offer?
Your voice, and your expression
are unique in all the world

You are a piece of the puzzle
You are needed
Listen to your Guides, your inner knowing
then Speak up

Become all that you are meant to be
Shine brightly

The time is now

Honor yourself
Honor others
Honor nature
Honor the trees
Honor the Sun
Honor the Moon

All are precious in our eyes
All are energy
Growing and evolving with you

Move with the energy
Feel the energy
Allow the flow

Recognize the synchronicities
Ask your questions
Receive the messages
Give messages

Create the world you want to see
Harmony

Let it be
Let it all be
All is as it should be
All is enfolding

You can't predict the future
You can't change the past

This moment is rich with infinite possibilities
This moment is everything

Tune into your heart
Let it expand
More light and love is pouring in
Healing
Evolving

Start anew from here

All is well
Stay the course
Ride the waves

Allow the new awareness to surface
Allow integration
Allow the process

All is happening for a reason for you
Your mind can't figure this out

Only YOUR soul understands this process

Let go and allow

The past is really finished
Gone
You are unable to move it
Change it

Let go
Feel the freedom
Soar

When you let go
You make space
for all that can be

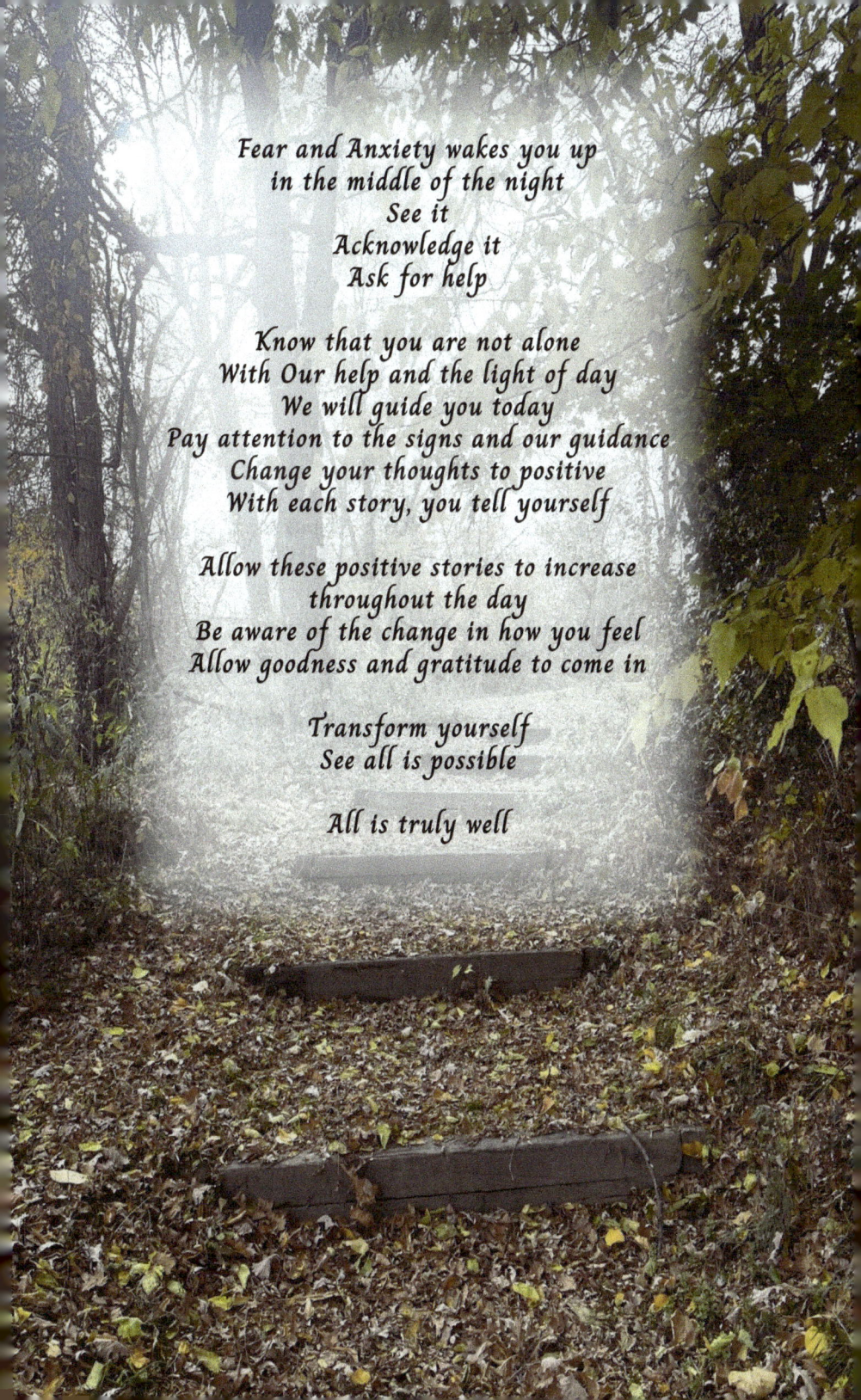

Mary Pat Magde

What does my body want me to know?

Be mindful when you eat
Stop
Slow down
Bless it
Savor it

I am strong
I am healing

As you heal your soul, accept all parts of yourself
Even the shadow parts

Yes, that was a good revelation you had yesterday

STOP, take a breath
check in with me before eating
before supplements
before exercising

I will communicate with you

We are a team on this earth

I'll help you be all that you can be

Release judgment and shame about me

Release worry, overthinking

I need time
It will happen

We will take these steps together
Use your body to show love
kiss and hug more
Enjoy walking in nature
each step on Mother Earth
seeing all the beauty
hearing the sounds

Feel the present moment through this body

I will lead you to a higher awareness through the present moment

I am so glad we are a team
much love
Smiles are from me too

Yes

Today
Focus on connection
Love
Appreciation

Enjoy

Your breath
A bit of light through the clouds
The colors you see all around you
Eye contact with another
A smile connection

Yes!

Move forward
Take a step
You've got this
See and feel your future

See all that you can be

Take the step forward

We see you shining brightly

We've known this all along

Now see yourself as we do

Much love

I saw you in a dream this morning
At first, I didn't recognize you
and then I did

I hugged you so tight and cried
Missing you here in physical form
The hug felt wonderful

Upon awakening, I understood
and know you are always with me
I just need to open my heart

No beloved person or pet is ever truly gone
They are with us
whispering to us
guiding us
and still loving us fully
We are a part of each other

It is only when our defenses are lowered,
we can feel them, hear them

I am grateful for this dream encounter
A wonderful reminder of
our connection to all,
always and forever

Be here NOW
Be fully HERE NOW
In this moment
In the silence and stillness
In the joy
In the sorrow
In all of it right now

Very slowly look around
What do you see?
What do you feel?

Allow and feel it all
Feelings do not last, positive or negative
Just feel
Be here NOW

Keep going

Regardless of the various messages you are all receiving

Remember - no need for comparison or judging

Each is evolving

All are learning from each other

You are a collective

All is well

Stand tall and strong
Be your own unique person

You have strength you don't see
but others do...
Trust your inner knowing

Take these steps forward

We applaud you
and see you shining fully

You are loved beyond measure

You are seen
You are heard
You are valuable
You are worthy
You are so precious
You are loved

You are needed here
Only you can shine your unique light
to others

You are never alone
We are with you
Feel the connection
to the Divine Source

Feel the peace, love, and joy
All is well

Some days are gray and cloudy
Some days are low-energy
Take the time to rest
and pull inward

All the ebbs and flows
are right where you need to be

Each has a purpose, a lesson,
a healing within

It's okay to pause
and just feel all the feelings
during these times

Feel fully
You'll know when it's complete

and then you can move to the
next phase of the journey

Honor it all

All in divine timing
All is well
Allow yourself to let go
and go with the flow

No need to push, defend, force, or argue
Be at peace within your heart

Wonder and Awe
of all the beauty in this world
Take it all in
Pause...Appreciate

Notice all the beauty within yourself
You are unique in all the world
Only you can be YOU!
The world needs you

We are all a part of ONENESS
Connected
Like how each puzzle piece
fits beautifully together

Your light and love
lifts the whole world

You are loved
You are LOVE

Inner Knowing: Heart Connections to the Divine Within

Arise and Awaken
to all that is
all that can be
and will be
The time is now to wake up
Remember who you truly are

You are here for a reason, a purpose
How can you shine your unique light and love to the world?

See all the beauty, wonder, and love that surrounds you

Be silent
Breathe
Go deep within your heart
Listen for the answers
of "Who am I?"

Turn off fear-promoting media
Let go of negativity, fear, and judgment now
Release all that no longer serves your highest good

Tune into your heart
All the answers are within

Do you see the path before you?
Where does it lead?
Take a few steps in your mind's eye
What do you see ahead?
Keep moving forward
As you move ahead, the scenes
can change to anything you want
How do you feel?
Now stand still
Breathe in this NOW moment
Be in this moment fully
Connect with the Peace within, Source
Breathe
How do you feel?
Awaken!

Go within my child
Go to the stillness within
Go to your breath
Simply in and out

Feel eternity in this now moment
Lovely
Ahh...

Today is a new beginning
This moment is new
and it's yours

Your choice...

Things, events, people's actions
are not what they seem
You may not always understand the purpose
Often things have to come to the surface
to be seen...
before it can clear...
and other choices can be made...

Be willing to see things differently

Hold space and love for all
It matters

Your inner peace and love
can be a balance
an anchor

What is your desire?
What do you want to create in this world?
What is waiting to be birthed from you?

Honor your uniqueness
Only you can bring this creation to the world
The world needs YOU

You have unique gifts and talents
Your own essence
Your Divine spark
Let it shine

It may be a smile towards a stranger
It may be an appreciation of a sunrise
or the beauty of nature
It may be a connection with someone
It may be rescuing and loving a cat or dog
It may be playing, laughing, dancing, hugging, singing
It may be a poem, art, or a book waiting to be written

Only you know, when you go deep inside

The time is now

Now
Now
Now
The present
Yes the gift

Thank you
Thank you
Thank you

Peace is within this moment
Happiness is within this moment
Joy is within this moment
Gratitude is within this moment
Understanding is within this moment

Eternity is within this moment
All timelines are within this moment

This moment
these seconds

Your choice

You are awakening a bit more each day,
each moment

You see
You understand
You know
You remember

All is as it should be
You are exactly where you need to be

Stand in the magic of this moment
This understanding of all

Observe
Allow
Shine

Your strength and wisdom come from the Divine within
All is being revealed a step at a time

You can now see how each experience
has led to the next

to the lessons
to the understanding
to the inner knowing

Gratitude
for the journey
Gratitude for
being here
and living fully
loving fully

Pause and see ALL
Feel all
BE ALL

We are revealing to you once again

Each person has their own journey
You cannot fix, change, or know
what's best for them

You walk your own journey
and continue to learn and evolve as well

They too are allowed time and space
to do the same

One way is not better than the other
All are walking and growing and evolving

Each a beautiful Divine Spark
See the Spark in all
people, animals, trees, flowers, rivers...
Everyone and Everything

Navigate from this understanding

Play
Experiment
Try something different
Out of the ordinary
Enjoy

Feel the newness
Feel the shift

Feel lighter
Enjoy!

Walk in nature slowly
Soak it in
You are one with nature
Bathe in it
Allow your cells to heal
Allow your heart to heal

Feel your body changing and healing
Digestion
Skin
Your mind
Heart
How you view the world
Allow us in to join with you

Love yourself completely
Love others

Be at peace

The time is now
Love. Love. Love.
All you need is love

Awaken from your slumber
Ease into life
Breathe

Feel the Peace

Things have changed
You can feel it

You may not be able to explain it all
But you can feel it deep in your soul

All is NEW

Drop into your heart,
your knowing...
to receive your wisdom
of your next step
in this moment

It's that simple

Compassion for ALL
since all people, animals, plants...are you
Each is a part of the collective
All are ONE

See yourself in All
See the Divine in ALL

Accept all
Accept all parts

Love ALL...

Oneness
No separation
All connected
All a part of each other
A beautiful intricate web

A ripple effect
What you say and do matters
it ripples through ALL

Speak love, kindness, wisdom
Allow your actions to reflect this

Show others the way
Be a light

Rise above to see the connections,
the oneness,
the beautiful endless infinite possibilities

We return to our deepest, highest self
We remember
We are all ONE

Look to nature for understanding
See the beauty
See it's strength

See the changes
See the evolution

See the endings
See the rebirth

Feel the rhythm
We have a rhythm
We have phases and different chapters on our journeys

What do you desire for this phase?

See it
Feel it
Create it
It's yours

Remember who you truly are

Arise, Awaken
See the new earth

See and feel all that is blooming now
Time for newness and change

Time for connectedness
cooperation
oneness
equality
and love

You are the creator

Everyone is unique
We each have our own way of being,
expressing ourselves in this world
A beautiful mosaic, kaleidoscope, ever-changing

The planet shines bright with each individual's light

Together, with collaboration,
we can create the world
we choose
One of collaboration, cooperation
Peace and love

Let us start with peace and love in our hearts
Let us live with peace and love in our hearts

Let our sparks of light shine brightly

We are the hope we have been waiting for

We remember our connectedness, our oneness

Go inward today
Before you look and act outward

How do you feel?
Is there anything that needs to be
cleared?
released?
accepted?
forgiven?
healed?
loved?
created?

Your body, your heart, can tell you what you need
Honor this

Honor yourself
with how you speak to yourself
And what you feed it
(food, conversations, digital information)

What's one area you can honor today?

Joy
Bliss
Pleasure
Laughter

Step INTO life
Your present moment

Beauty
Gratitude

Healing
Forgiving
Releasing
Surrendering
Allowing

Loving
Being ALIVE

BEING

Love
Love
Love
All you need is love

Love for self
Fill yourself up
Then you can share love with others

Look into your heart
What do you need to release?
Forgive?
Accept?
Surrender to?
So you can truly love yourself?

Allow this process
Notice in the
NOW moment
Do you feel any restrictions?
Blocks?
Fear?
Anger?
Feel it
Accept it
Love it
It's all a part of you
Then release it

This allows the space for Love to flood in

This is a continuous process
We are forever evolving into LOVE
Being a conduit of love

This is why we are here

You are not lost
the momentum is still moving forward
even if you can't always feel it

Pause
Breathe

Notice how quickly you can observe
transmute a situation or feeling
Release

Yes it's all happening

So wonderful
We are reminding you
that where you are today
is eons away from a year ago
a week ago
yesterday
a moment ago

All changes in a moment
with the simple emotion of love
the knowing of love
of being love

Mary Pat Magde

Your heart
The Center of it all

Contains memories
hurt, sadness

Shines out of your smile
your Love

The home of your Soul

Where in silence
you find Yourself again

You find your Connection

You can plant seeds of your wishes

Where we are all the same
Connected as One

Surrender

Ride the roller coaster of life
Dips happen
Then you are heading back up again

Observe

Each dip and rise
is just a bit different than before

You are learning and evolving

Be curious about it all

Allow the emotions

You are here to experience it all

Relax
Feel the warm embrace of my light today
We are always with you
Open
Allow
Surrender
Receive
Appreciate
Elevate

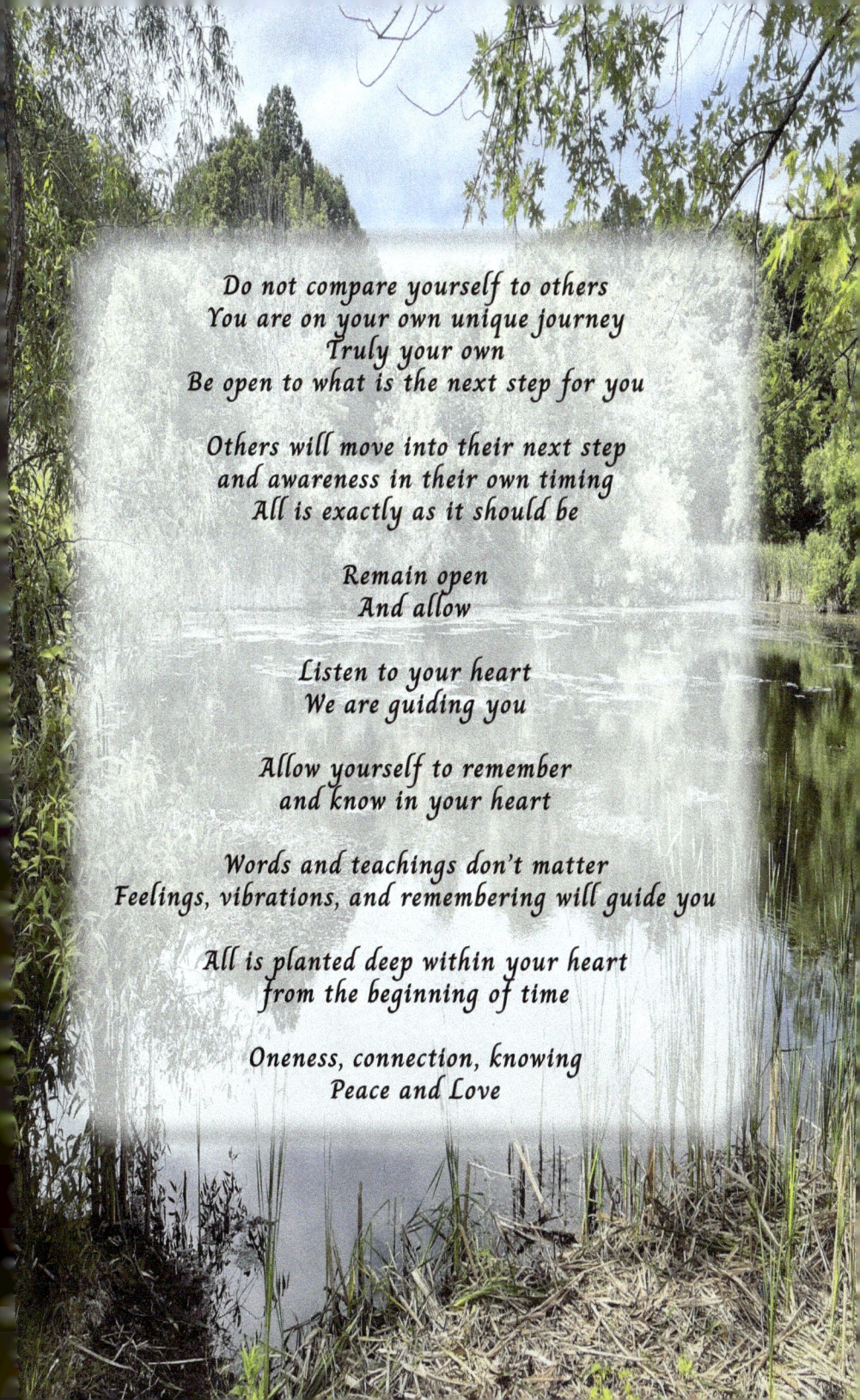

Do not compare yourself to others
You are on your own unique journey
Truly your own
Be open to what is the next step for you

Others will move into their next step
and awareness in their own timing
All is exactly as it should be

Remain open
And allow

Listen to your heart
We are guiding you

Allow yourself to remember
and know in your heart

Words and teachings don't matter
Feelings, vibrations, and remembering will guide you

All is planted deep within your heart
from the beginning of time

Oneness, connection, knowing
Peace and Love

Breathe in...
Breathe out...

Breathe in...
Breathe out...

Breathe in...
Breathe out...

What do you see?

What do you hear?

What do you feel?

Be here now

Every moment is sacred

Shining your light, what does that mean?
Helping others, helping the world, humanity,
what does that look like?

Each person can connect, align
with their hearts light,
the Spark of Divinity within.

You came here for a purpose.
You are needed and valued.
Be you!
Share your unique talents and gifts...
art, gardening, your humor,
your smile with strangers,
your patience, your love...
Shine out!

How can we assist others or world situations?
Simply hold the positive vision
of all that can be.
See individuals and
groups, humanity connecting
with their own sparks
of Divinity within
and acting and being in their highest self.

See ALL in its highest form.

We are all one.

You are seen
You are known

You are seen as a Divine Spark of God
Regardless of your actions
your trials
your shame
your growth
or triumphs

You are complete

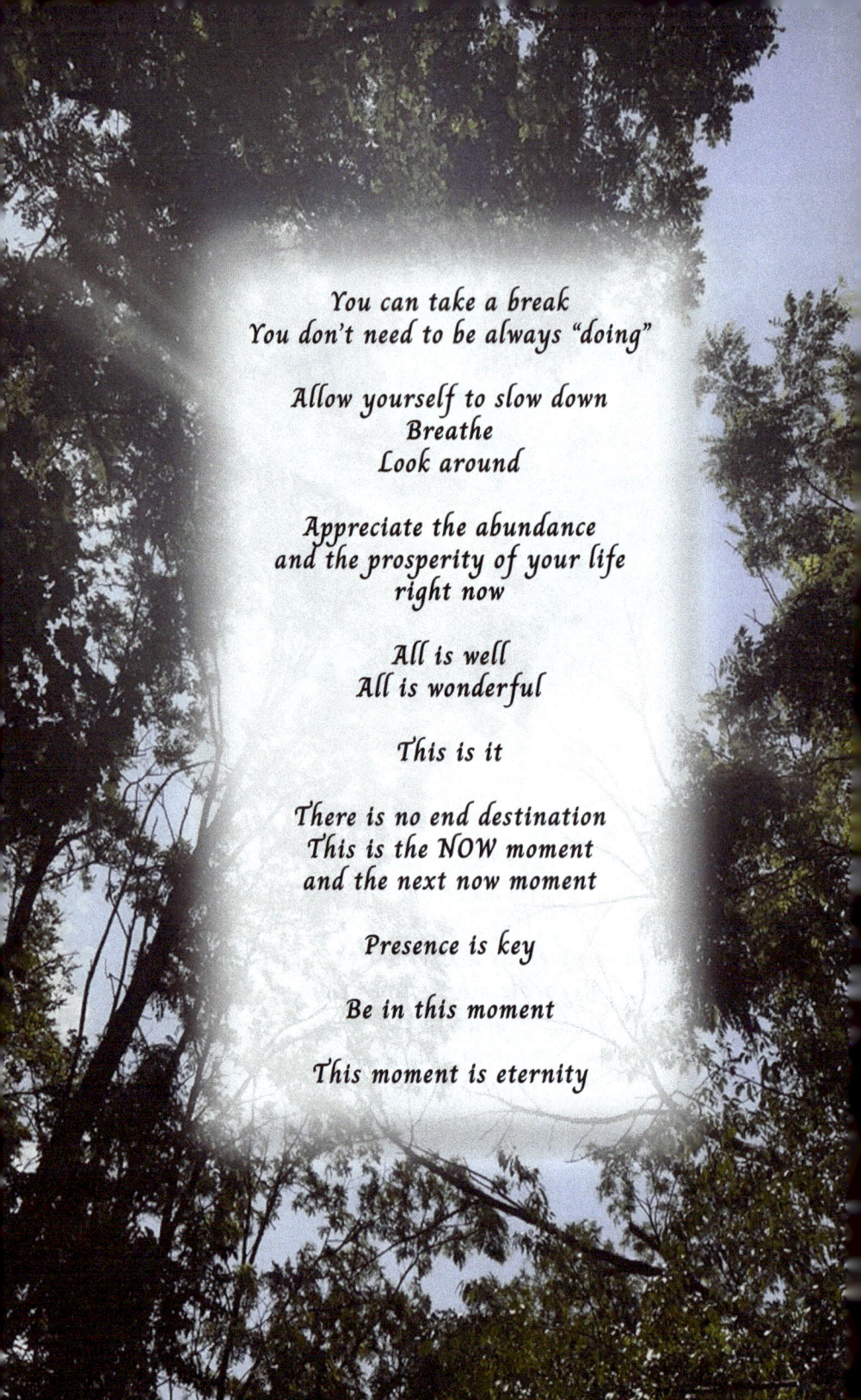

You can take a break
You don't need to be always "doing"

Allow yourself to slow down
Breathe
Look around

Appreciate the abundance
and the prosperity of your life
right now

All is well
All is wonderful

This is it

There is no end destination
This is the NOW moment
and the next now moment

Presence is key

Be in this moment

This moment is eternity

Peace
Peace within

Joy
Joy within

Self-compassion
Acceptance

All are available to you
right now
Join with them
Be them

Be Love
Be the Light

Release the fear
don't ignore it
Feel it and release

Recenter into your peaceful heart

You are the world, the universe

Change is coming
It is necessary to be seen and released

Allow
Allow
Allow

You can focus on yourself
Release and allow

Love unconditionally

Be at peace
Find your center
in the midst of the storm

Be an anchor for others

We are with you
We are with you
We are with you

Walk every day in nature
Ground yourself

Share your gifts, your light

Yes, this is your purpose
We love you
We love you
We love you
You and all the precious ones

You can do this
Keep walking forward through the storm

Tell others you love them
Be with people
Share your light and love

We are infinite beings
Your core
Your soul

Breathe into the magnificent eternity,
Divine Source
That is your constant
your anchor

Read this again and again

That is all for now
Love always and forever

Be the stillness
Pause
between breaths
between thoughts

Pause before speaking
before acting

Allow wonder to emerge

Discover

What if?
What if when I experience
any fear,
insecurity,
doubt,
pain...

Instead of running from it
or hiding from it
or burying it

I sit with it?
See it as just another temporary part of me?
Maybe even visualize...
what age is that part of me
Or maybe
see where I feel it in my body?

AND THEN
just sit with it
feel it
welcome it
Hug and LOVE that part of me
Release resistance
and show kindness to this part of me?

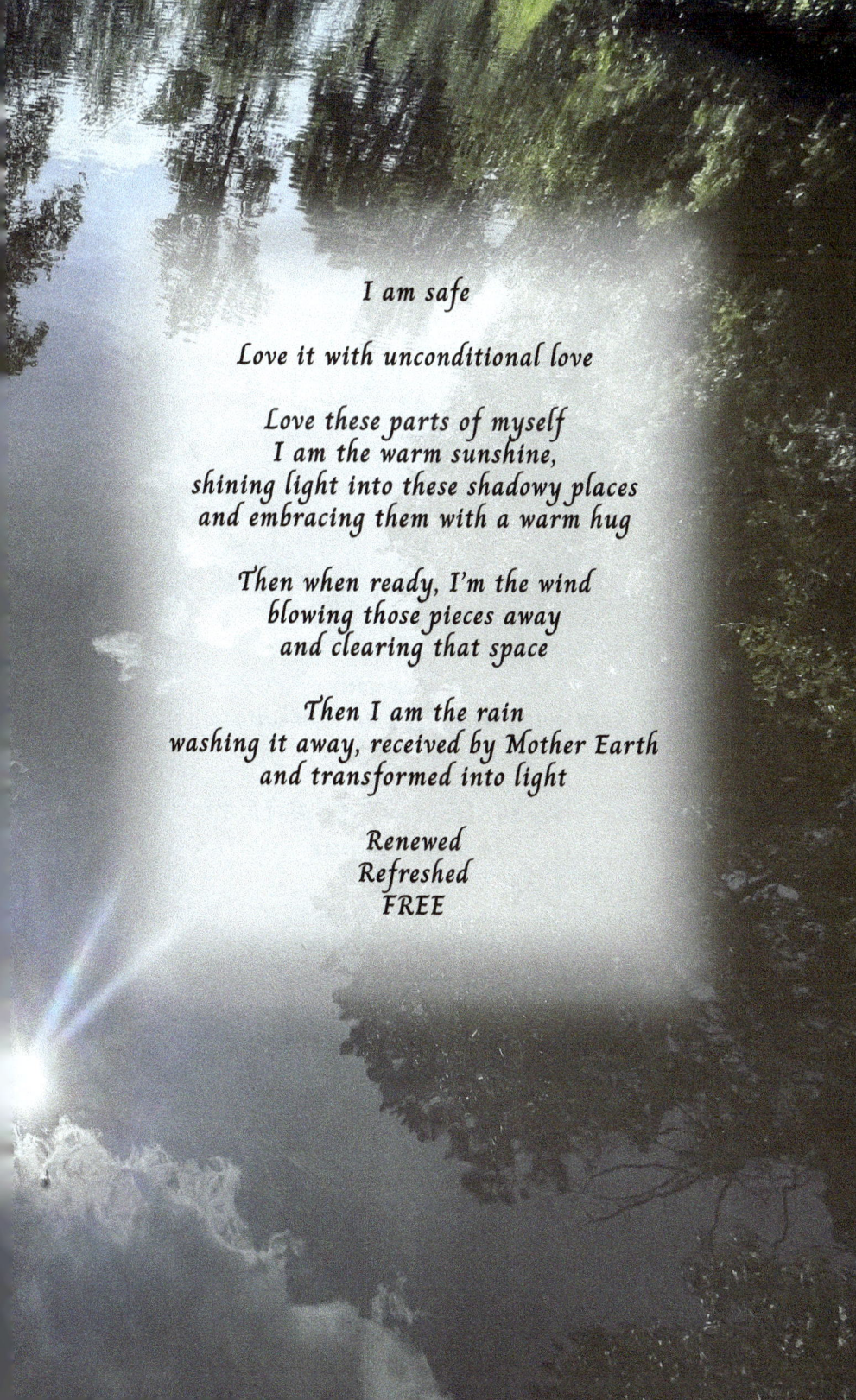

I am safe

Love it with unconditional love

Love these parts of myself
I am the warm sunshine,
shining light into these shadowy places
and embracing them with a warm hug

Then when ready, I'm the wind
blowing those pieces away
and clearing that space

Then I am the rain
washing it away, received by Mother Earth
and transformed into light

Renewed
Refreshed
FREE

We love you
Keep going with your daily meditation
and channeling

See the beauty in the world
In people, nature
In all

Slow your breathing
to be present

Each next moment is a surprise
Lean into it

Allow and BE

Yes

All is well

Love and Peace
the foundation of all

Look inward first
Do you forgive yourself?
Can you love yourself unconditionally?
...yes, with all your imperfections?

It all begins with your inner journey

We can't truly love or serve others
until we love ourselves

You are LOVE
You are LOVED

See yourself as a young child, innocent
Love and hug them

You are a unique light in this world
You are needed

Claim yourself
Claim your voice
Claim your truth

You are loved fully for who you are
all parts of you, the light and shadows
without judgment
Just LOVED

Feel this love
Feel this peace

Inner Knowing: Heart Connections to the Divine Within

Rest

Needed

Changes happening on the physical, mental, emotional, and spiritual levels

Surrender and Allow

You'll know when this phase is done and you are ready to move forward

All is well

*Observe
Just observe*

*Judge nothing...
yourself, people, events, circumstances*

*Be mindful
Detach
Judgment free*

*Just take a deep breath
Pause*

Acceptance

Releasing and Letting Go
a natural cycle

Take pause today
and think of what you can release
that no longer serves you

A day to go inward...
Good Friday reflection
Full Moon releasing
Spring cleaning
of physical, emotional, mental, and spiritual stuff

So needed to make room for what
can come next into your life

Rebirth!

Mary Pat Magde

What does it mean we are all one?
We are spiritual beings living a human experience
Our souls, our divine spirit, are all one
My spirit is no different than yours
Your spirit is no different than mine

We are all on our soul's journey
All learning lessons and growing

You can awaken to this connection
The veil has been lifted now
Awaken to the concept
that "anything is possible"

Awaken to the alignment of your divine spirit
Rise above with this new perspective
See the glorious Union of all

When I was taking a walk out in nature yesterday,
I asked the sky, trees,
grass, nature, Mother Earth,
what wisdom do you have for us?

Notice we are always changing
We change
You see some of the changes
Each minute is new

You change minute by minute too

We also change on a microscopic cellular level
And we change on an energetic level

We give and receive energy
Keep walking in nature

Your energy matters
You can raise your vibration
(smile, gratitude, joy, appreciate nature [us], love)
It can have a collective ripple effect on the world

If you find yourself fearful, angry,
hopeless, or anxious in low-vibration
Try to find one small thing to appreciate –
a bird, the blue sky, the taste of your
favorite food, a joke, a smile from a
stranger, a soft cozy texture, a favorite song,
a pleasing scent, etc.

We love you

So many possibilities
All is opening up now
A new frontier

Unknown yet trusting
Deep knowing and believing

Like a flower blossoming in Spring,
we are blossoming into a new life
a new perspective
a new truth now

Let the light continue to feed us
to grow
to open
to bloom
to shine

Silence
Turn off the external noise
Breathe deeply
and find the silence within
Your soul

Then you can know your inner wisdom
the Divine Spark within

Guiding you
Shining the light for you

Discovering your true essence
and all you are meant to be in this world

You are unique in all the world
Let your spirit dance
Let your spirit shine

You are so loved and cherished

It's okay to have times of shadow
It's okay to be like a turtle and pull inside yourself
It's okay to not follow your routine
It's okay to not be perfect
It's okay to not know who you are

With all the kaleidoscope of emotions
that can arise:
doubt, frustration, anxiety, worry, fear,
sadness, unworthiness
as well as
hope, love, joy, bliss
Let them flow through you
Don't capture them and hold them
Simply feel them, fully,
then release

As you release the density of heavy feelings,
it leaves a space
a glorious space
to allow NEW
to allow more light to come in

Continue to clear your clutter
(material, physical, mental, emotional, and spiritual)
to allow light and expansion

This is the process now

You are a Divine Being living in a human body

Evolving and ever-expanding

You are not crazy
Yes these things are really happening
and you can feel yourself changing
and the world changing
even if you don't know why or
have words to describe this process

Something is different now
...each day
Do you see it?
Do you see the good?
Do you see the beauty?
Do you see the Divine in each person?
Do you see things a bit more from a higher
perspective?

The old ways and beliefs are falling away...
Making room for remembering
your True Self now

We are here
We are always here, sweet child
Ask us anything
Ask for guidance and support
We are available 24/7
Yes for those middle-of-the-night worries too

If you feel you have been pulled off your course
with old thinking, emotions
Simply stop, breathe, and recenter yourself
All is well

Grey and cloudy this morning
Then the sun came out
and your mind changed quickly

Same with changing your thoughts and emotions
It can be that quick
As the rising and shining of the sun

Let the light shine on your darkness

We love you

What does this magnificent tree want me to know?
I am standing alone in a field
And from your viewpoint
I look like I'm alone
No one else is close by
But in reality, under the earth
and connected to the earth,
I am connected to
ALL
Just as you are
Even
when you sometimes think you are alone
Or standing in your own confidence...
You will always be connected to Mother Earth,
the sky, and the Universe just as
a tree
Just as I am a tree

*Be like a snowflake
Floating with the wind
Each is unique...*

*Be like a puppy
Everything is new!
Exciting
And sometimes scary*

Jump, run, and play in this life

Today be in the moment
Really be in the moment

When you catch yourself in the past or future,
bring yourself back

Take a breath, look around, see, feel, taste, hear, touch...
Awwwwww...beautiful, right?

This moment won't happen again...
We don't want you to miss it
Just like that beautiful sunrise this morning

Enjoy sweet child

All is well

Let go of old ways
of being, thinking, and behaving
that no longer serve you
Release

See all you imagine for your future
in this present moment
Feel the joy, wonder, and gratitude

Take the next step

Allow your spirit to shine

Let it shine to all those around you,
to strangers
to the world

Let your heart and soul expand
Love and joy are contagious

Create this moment, yourself
and the world with your love

Good morning
It's a new day

Yes, each day, each moment is new
Isn't that glorious?

A choice in each moment to be present

So many possibilities
So much to enjoy
So much to experience

So much life

Yes, you are alive
and that is a gift today

Breathe it all in
Enjoy

Breathe out love

Feel your connection
to everyone, everything

We are all ONE

The time is now

All is well dear child
All is truly well

Awareness of your shadows is all part of learning to
accept yourself, all of you

Stay aware and conscious
don't hide or bury these parts

Let them come out and love on them
Yes, love transmutes all

This is all part of this journey

You are not alone, we are with you
Call on us for support at any time

Feel our love,
allow yourself to feel this deep love for yourself

Yes, LOVE is the answer

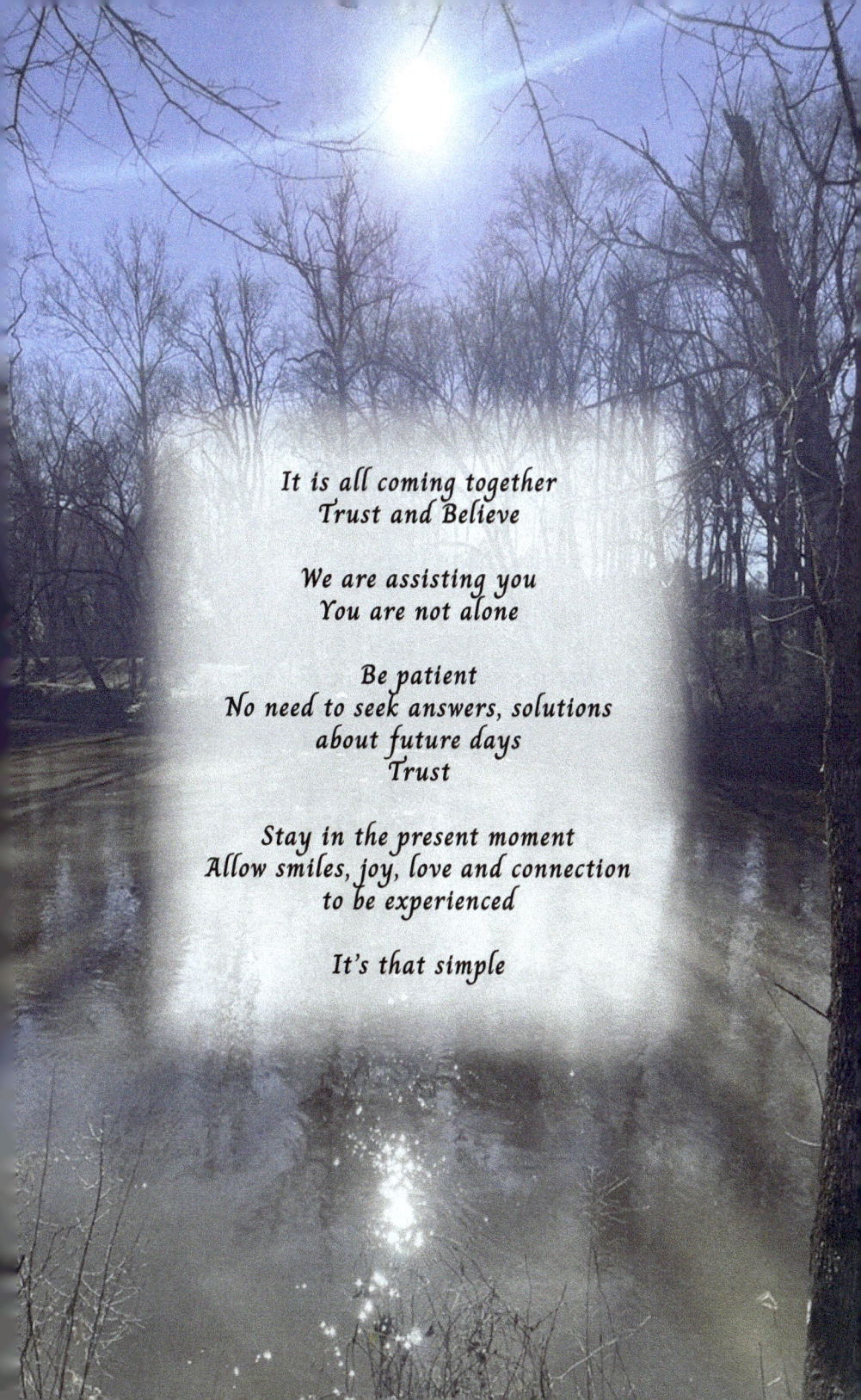

It is all coming together
Trust and Believe

We are assisting you
You are not alone

Be patient
No need to seek answers, solutions
about future days
Trust

Stay in the present moment
Allow smiles, joy, love and connection
to be experienced

It's that simple

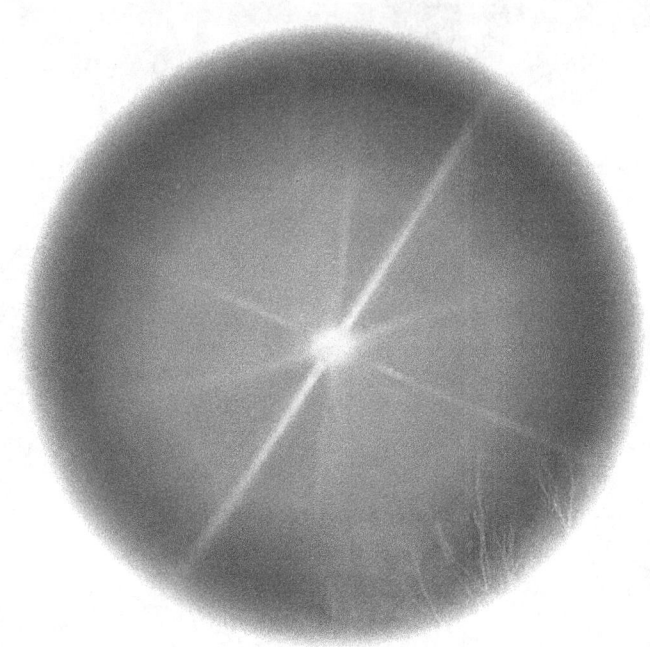

Who am I?
Not the person I was in my past
I see the past and own it
but it is no longer me

Who am I now
in this moment?

Not my name
Not my career
Not my interests
Not my role in life or in my family

I am a spiritual being
Just as you are

I see the Divine in you

The Divine within me
bows to the same Divine
within you

Namaste

Rest
Quiet
Sleep
All nourishing for your soul's transformation

As you awake
All things are made new

You have arrived
The time is now

Glorious gratitude to be alive

Creation is yours
Transformation is possible

Dance
Celebrate

Continue with your daily meditation
It takes practice and time
BUT it is not work
and there is no right or wrong
Just do it
Simple

You are looking for your purpose
Looking for your next step
Which course or path to follow
(Mindfulness training, Angel card reading,
painting, or soul sister group, etc.)

It is simply to BE
as other guides have shared

No need for any courses or training at this time

Meditate and channel
Read the Channeling group

Keep it simple
No stress

Tune in to life
Walk in nature
Observe
Connect
Marvel

We love you

*Pause
Yes...Pause
so powerful*

*Pause
between breaths
to find the stillness inside*

*Pause
to listen*

*Pause
before speaking*

*Pause
before eating*

*Pause
before acting*

Pause

You can begin again today
this moment

Reset

Let go of old baggage
Release
and be reborn in this moment

The day opens like a flower
Opens to the light

Light pours in
Restores
Nourishes

Stand tall in your knowing

Reconnect to yourself
your soul
and reconnect to all

Yes, We are One

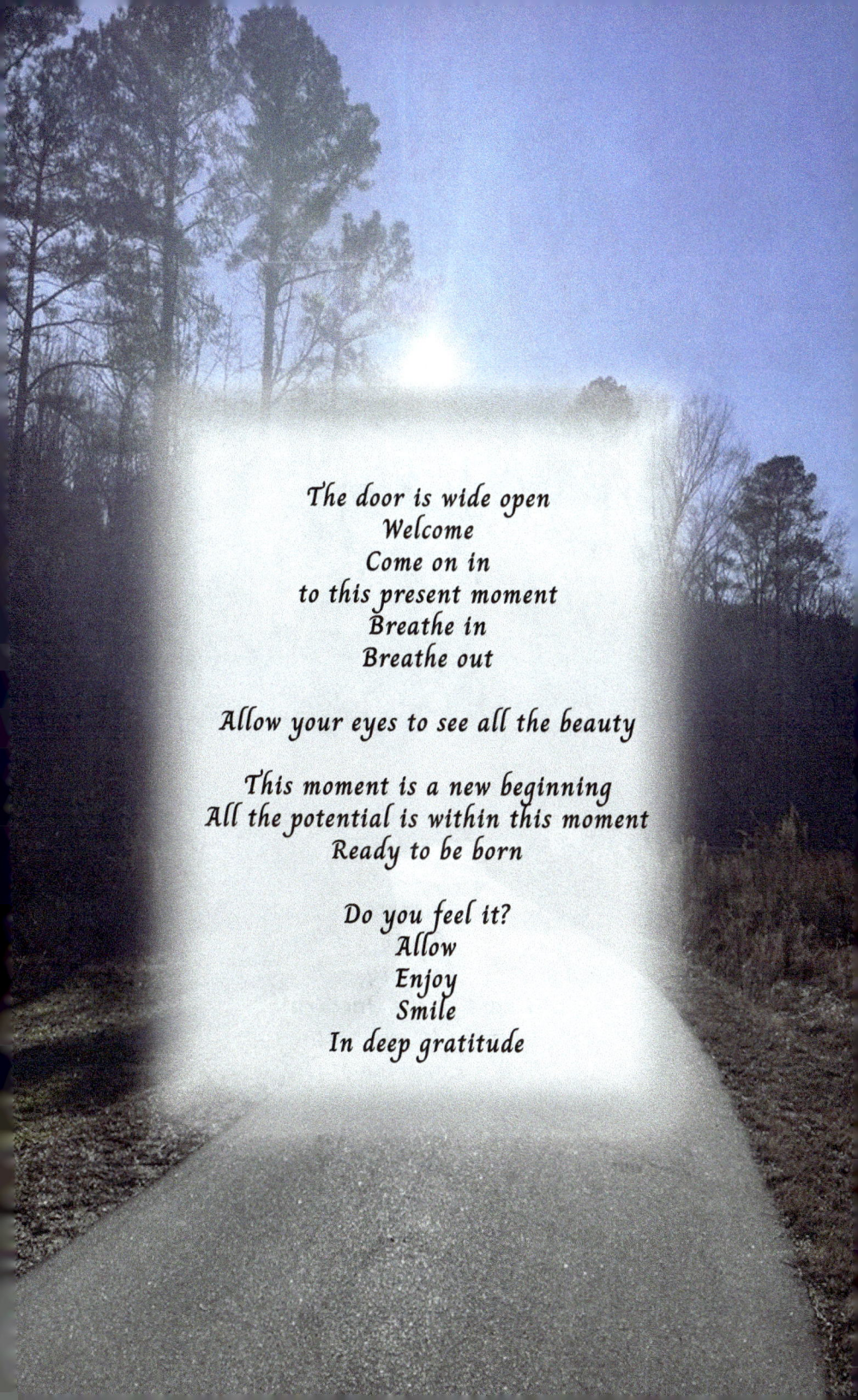

Oneness
Truth
Polarity
All part of the One Truth
Living in our truth
Truly Honoring others

What connects us all?

Hello
Welcome back
You are always welcomed back to your connection to us
We love you dearly

A day of rest prepares you for the next leap

You are exactly where you need to be

Today is a brand new day

See it as a beautiful gift
Present

Observe with wonder as each moment unfolds

That is it, that simple

All is well
All continues to be well

You can try hard things
Move out of your comfort zone
and find new discoveries
of self and life

We encourage you to
step through the doorway

We are here with you
You are not alone

Keep taking steps forward
There is so much to discover
Beyond what you can even imagine

Welcome, dear child.
Yes, we are with you as you question yourself

We are with each of you, so why
wouldn't we be with you every minute,
every day, forever and ever?

Take a deep breath

Yes, now you feel it

All is well

Release your fears, worries, and old stories

See your life, every aspect of it from above, like we see you

Today is going to be a marvelous, glorious day!

I asked...How can I help and support others?

Remember they are on their own journey,
their own path that is uniquely theirs
You don't need to fix it or change it

Just sit with them, be with them
send them light, love, and healing from your infinite heart

Trust that they will find their way
just as you have
Trust
Truly trust this

We love you
All is well

Rebalance
After a time of unrest, challenge, struggle
Take the time
to rest and reset

Today is a new opportunity
to step into your Divine Knowing

Feel it
Be it

Connect with your Inner Wisdom
Rediscover Oneness
Remembrance
Love
Returning to "home" within your heart
You know this

You are not alone
Ask for guidance
You are loved and cherished always

All is well
Anything is possible
Step into your power

You are exactly where you need to be today
You are loved beyond measure
You have grown, expanded
and we have witnessed it

There is no race or endpoint to rush to

Be here now in the moment

Slow down

Feel the peace within

Lessons from trees
If you look around in the winter months
it looks like some trees are sleeping
dormant or very quiet
Yet there is still lots happening inside

Other trees, like evergreens,
don't look like they have changed much on the outside
Yet there is still lots happening inside

Some trees sustain injuries or wounds
yet continue to grow
Some trees are held back by vines
yet consistently grow against all odds
There are trees that stand alone
and trees that grow in groups
helping each other

Trees are great teachers for us

Trees have different shapes, sizes, qualities
…different life spans

Trees have different ways they can contribute
Yet all are connected with roots
to Mother Earth
All connected in an underground network
All one
As we are

No one tree is any more special than another
Each has a beautiful essence inside
regardless of what we see with our eyes

All interconnected

Listen to your heart
Hear us as we whisper to you
throughout the day

Share your day with us
Everything

Take pause, breathe, and tune in

You have all of our support
no need to struggle on your own

Open and receive

Allow

We love you

Enjoy...Joy

About the Author

Mary Pat Magde is a seeker, deeply curious about life and spiritual development. She is the author of "Inner Knowing - Heart Connections to the Divine Within," which features channeled poetry and photographs.

Throughout her personal journey, Mary Pat has delved into various spiritual practices, starting from traditional paths to meditation, angels, channeling, and Transference Healing. Her experiences of walking in nature, feeling a connection to the trees, and appreciating the wonder and beauty around her have all played a significant role in her spiritual exploration. This debut book captures her inward journey through her poetry and photography.

In her leisure time, Mary Pat enjoys hiking trails and connecting with nature across the four seasons in New York State. She cherishes moments spent in retirement with her husband, children, grandchildren, family, friends, and her loyal dogs, Jax (Collie) and Mickey (Sheltie).

Mary Pat Magde

www.ingramcontent.com/pod-product-compliance
Lightning Source LLC
Chambersburg PA
CBHW050833160426
43192CB00010B/2006